Outdoor Sportsmanship

By Christopher Forest

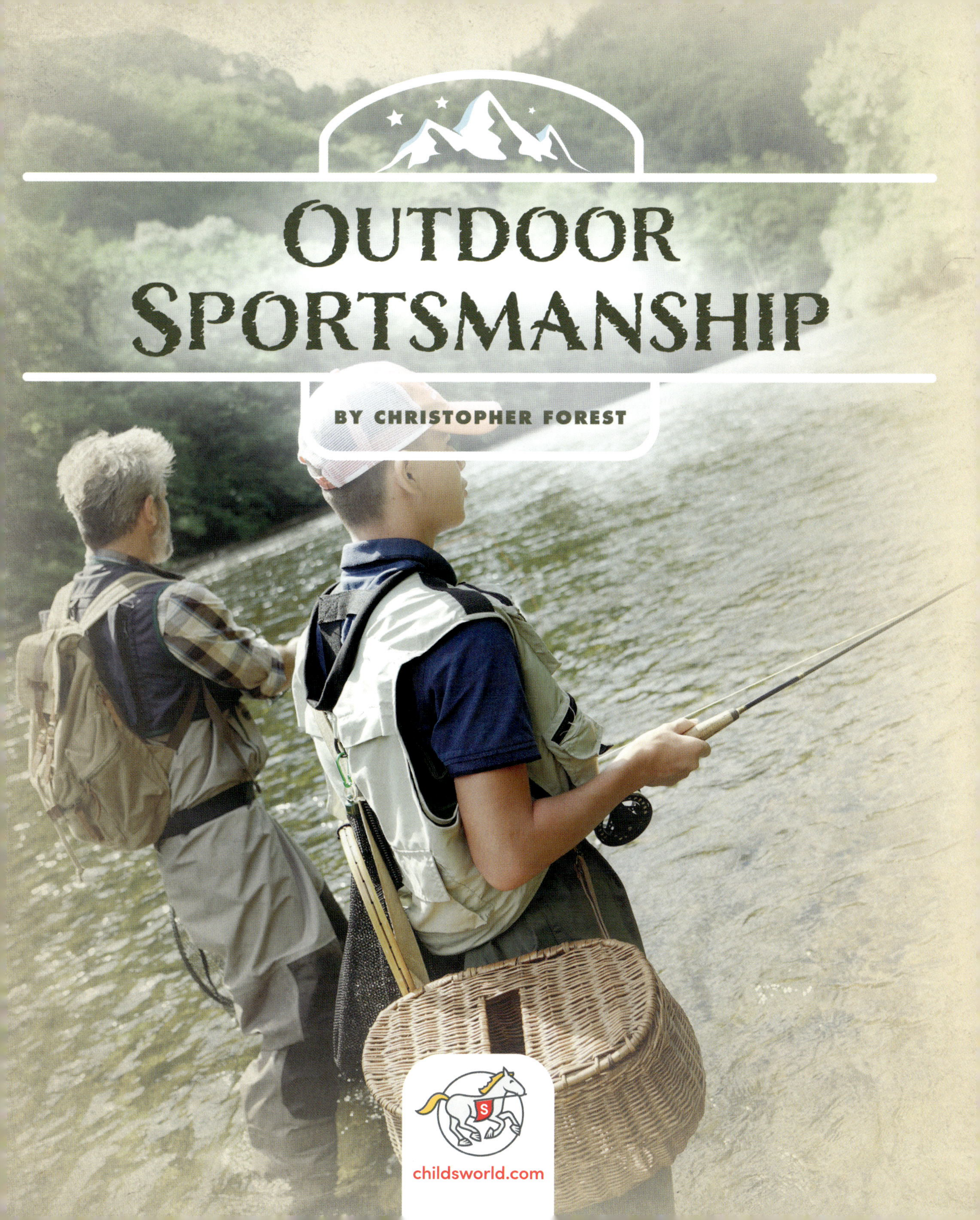

childsworld.com

Published by The Child's World®
800-599-READ • www.childsworld.com

Photography Credits
Photographs ©: Shutterstock Images, cover, 1, 11; Mary Violet/iStockphoto, 5; Keith Szafranski/iStockphoto, 7; iStockphoto, 9, 15; Red Line Editorial, 10; Brian Sevald/iStockphoto, 13; Everett Collection/Shutterstock Images, 17; Jack Sooksan/iStockphoto, 18; Magnus Moller/iStockphoto, 20; Hero Images Inc/Shutterstock Images, 21

ISBN Information
9781503869783 (Reinforced Library Binding)
9781503881037 (Portable Document Format)
9781503882348 (Online Multi-user eBook)
9781503883659 (Electronic Publication)

LCCN 2022951202

Printed in the United States of America

ABOUT THE AUTHOR

Christopher Forest is a middle school teacher in Massachusetts. He enjoys writing books for all ages. He has written nonfiction and fiction stories, articles, and novels for adults and children. In his spare time, he enjoys watching sports, playing guitar, reading, and spending time outdoors.

Contents

CHAPTER ONE

Sportsmanship in the Wild

It was a cool summer morning at Diamond Lake. Jessie, Carlos, and their father were just waking up at their campsite. It was the perfect day for fishing.

They got dressed and tidied up the campsite. Jessie and Carlos built a campfire to cook breakfast. After they finished eating, Jessie carefully put out the campfire. She knew it was important to make sure the fire didn't spread while they were out fishing. Putting out the fire would help prevent wildfires.

Jessie, Carlos, and their father gathered their fishing gear and loaded it into their rowboat. After everyone put on their life jackets, they hopped into the boat. Their father steered them to a good fishing spot.

Jessie and Carlos prepared their fishing rods. They checked that their **lures** were securely tied, so they would not pop off in a fish's mouth. Jessie and Carlos also made sure they weren't sitting too close together. They didn't want to accidentally hit each other while casting their lines. Then they cast their lines into the water.

People should follow all campfire safety rules in their area. To properly put out a campfire, people should pour water over the fire and stir the ashes until the firepit is no longer hot.

Soon, Jessie's line gave a slight tug. "I think I got something," she said. She reeled in her catch. It was a trout! She gently guided the fish into a net. Jessie and Carlos carefully inspected the trout, keeping the net in the water. To protect the fish, they needed to limit the amount of time it was outside of the water. The fish looked smaller than Jessie expected. Their father measured it. In order to keep the fish, they had to make sure it matched their state's legal size limit for trout.

The fish measured 18 inches (46 cm). "I'm afraid this one is too small," said their father. Jessie was disappointed, but she knew it was important to follow the rules. Releasing the fish would help keep the trout population in the lake **stable**. Jessie carefully removed the hook from the fish's mouth to avoid injuring it. Then she released the fish back into the lake.

A responsible **angler** like Jessie shows good sportsmanship outdoors. Many people enjoy outdoor sports such as fishing and hunting. But they must be respectful while engaging in these activities. This means treating wildlife, land, and other people fairly and respectfully. By demonstrating sportsmanship, people make it possible for everyone to enjoy the great outdoors.

When handling fish, an angler must be gentle. He should carefully remove the hook and avoid squeezing the fish too tightly. This helps keep the fish from being injured.

CHAPTER TWO

PLAYING BY THE RULES

Hunters and anglers should understand all the rules and regulations that apply to outdoor spaces. **State agencies** run state parks and wildlife reserves, or areas where animals are protected. State agencies make rules about how and when people can use these outdoor spaces. They also decide which activities are allowed in these locations. For instance, Yellowstone National Park has a rule about putting out campfires after using them.

People must also get permission to hunt or fish. In most states, people who want to do these activities must purchase a fishing **permit** or hunting license. They can buy licenses at outdoor equipment stores. While many people enjoy outdoor activities in public places, some land is privately owned. Hunting and fishing may not be allowed on private property. Sometimes people must get the landowner's permission before using private land.

Hunters should be aware of hunting rules in their states, too. Different states have different hunting seasons. Hunting season is the time of year when people can legally hunt certain animals.

Visitors at state parks, national parks, and other outdoor spaces should follow all rules. Hikers, for example, should stay on marked trails to avoid harming plants or wildlife.

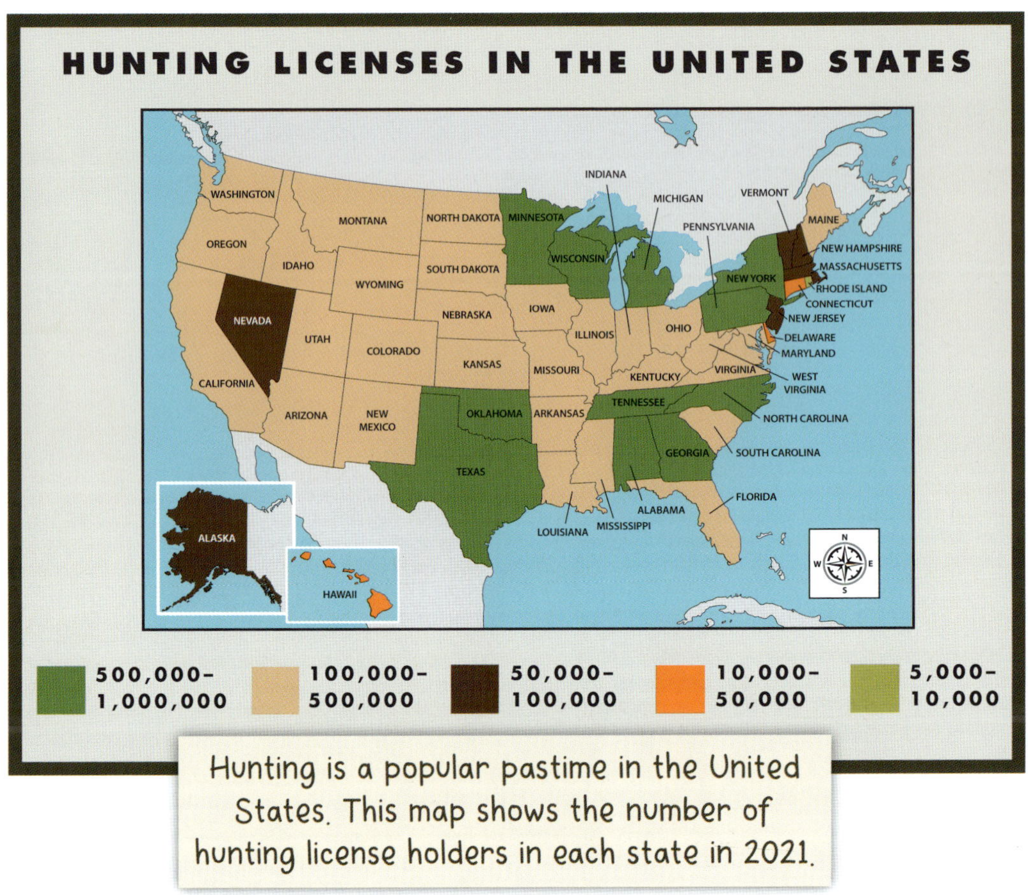

Hunting is a popular pastime in the United States. This map shows the number of hunting license holders in each state in 2021.

Hunting seasons are scheduled around times when animals mate and have offspring. This keeps hunters from shooting females at times when they might have babies with them. That way, mothers can raise their young safely. Hunting seasons are often in the fall, when animals are grown up and can survive on their own.

Many states set bag limits for hunters. These are limits on how many animals a person is allowed to hunt. Bag limits help prevent overhunting, which could cause some animal populations to drop.

Some states have rules about when and where certain hunting weapons can be used. For deer hunting, bowhunting season may be separate from firearm season.

Some states also set size limits for animals. These limits might involve the size of an animal, such as a fish's length. Or they might have to do with the size of an animal's features, such as a deer's antlers. In some places, a deer's antlers must be a certain width or have a specific number of points in order to be hunted. Otherwise, the deer is too young to hunt.

Some states require hunters and anglers to report the animals they catch or kill. State agencies receive these reports. They use this information to manage animal populations in the state. This helps prevent overhunting and overfishing.

CHAPTER THREE

OUTDOOR ETHICS

Hunters and anglers should follow **ethical** practices in the outdoors. Some people hunt animals for food. When they make a kill, they are careful not to waste any part of the animal. Other people hunt for fun. Shooting large animals may be rewarding. Hunters sometimes keep parts of hunted animals, such as antlers, to display in their homes as trophies. Trophies show off a hunter's success. Whether hunting for food or sport, people should always follow a code of conduct that respects wildlife.

Hunters and anglers can practice ethical behavior by making sure animals do not suffer. When hunting, people should try to aim accurately and make clean shots. These are shots that hit important organs in an animal's body, causing the animal to die quickly. The animal suffers less this way. Hunters should also avoid using hunting techniques that cause animals stress. One harmful method is called dog hunting. This involves chasing bears with dogs.

People should follow the rules of fair chase, too. They should avoid using hunting methods that give them an unfair or cruel advantage over animals. They should also obey all hunting laws in their area. Some hunting methods, such as baiting, are illegal.

Whether hunting with bows or guns, all hunters should practice aiming accurately. Beginners can take hunter education courses or practice at shooting ranges.

WHERE DO HUNTING RULES COME FROM?

Hunting rules usually come from the office of a state wildlife management agency. These agencies have sessions where people discuss rules and regulations. Many hunting and fishing groups support new rules or rule changes. Rules that are passed often benefit hunters, anglers, and animals. In the end, state agencies decide which rules go into effect in each state. This is why different states have different rules.

Baiting involves leaving out large amounts of food to lure animals to an area. Many states outlaw baiting because it can harm animals and cause pollution. People should also never hunt animals in fenced-in areas. They should only hunt or fish in natural environments where animals are free to roam.

People should know how to use guns, bows, and fishing rods safely, too. They can take hunter education courses to learn how to use these tools properly. This helps people avoid injuring themselves or others while outdoors. People should respect other hunters and anglers, too. If another person is closer to an animal, it is polite to allow that person to catch the animal. By practicing ethical behaviors, hunters and anglers can make sure everyone has a memorable experience in the outdoors.

Anglers can respect others by sharing fishing areas and making sure everyone has enough space to cast their lines.

CHAPTER FOUR

Being Conservation-Minded

Hunters and anglers have a long history of being conservation-minded. This means they respect wildlife and the environment. One famous conservationist was President Theodore Roosevelt. He enjoyed hunting, but he also believed in protecting the environment. As president, Roosevelt helped protect more than 230 million acres (93 million ha) of land, establishing national parks and wildlife preserves.

Roosevelt encouraged Americans to protect the outdoors. By being conservation-minded, people can accomplish this. They can care for the environment and respect wildlife. People who are conservation-minded know they have a duty to take care of the wilderness for future generations.

One way to be conservation-minded is to use nonlead bullets while hunting. Lead is a poisonous metal that can make animals sick. Animals might accidentally eat lead **shot** left on the ground.

In 1903, President Theodore Roosevelt visited Yosemite. The trip inspired him to establish national parks, monuments, wildlife refuges, and national forests.

Yellowstone National Park is famous for its hot springs and wildlife. To be respectful and responsible, visitors should stay on trails, avoid getting too close to hot springs, and keep a safe distance from animals.

Or they might eat the remains of animals that have been shot with lead bullets. In the outdoors, hunters must clean up after themselves. They should never leave litter or hunting equipment behind. Many hunters and anglers try to leave the land exactly as they found it. For instance, hunters must be careful when field dressing animals. This involves removing organs from an animal's body before transporting it home. Some states have rules about the proper disposal of animal remains.

Conservation-minded hunters and anglers understand the role they play in the **ecosystem**. By hunting and fishing during the correct seasons and following bag limits, people help keep animal populations stable. They make sure that populations do not become too small or large. Hunters and anglers impact an ecosystem's **food web**, too. They may remove predators from the environment. Predators feed on other types of animals.

NATIONAL PARKS

Each year, millions of people visit national parks all over the United States. The first national park was created in 1872. It was Yellowstone National Park, which is located in Wyoming, Idaho, and Montana. Since then, the government has opened many national parks. Lots of parks allow hunting and fishing. The National Park Service hopes that by allowing hunting and fishing in these areas, people will develop an appreciation for the outdoors. It hopes people will help conserve the land and keep animal populations balanced.

Hunters can protect animals by field dressing their kills properly. This keeps the land clean and prevents animals from eating traces of lead in animal remains.

Animals hunted by predators are called prey. Hunting predators can help increase some prey animal populations.

Following rules and making ethical decisions in the outdoors are the hallmarks of good outdoor sportsmanship. By upholding this code of sportsmanship, people can enjoy the outdoors responsibly. They can protect the land for future generations.

Experienced hunters, anglers, and outdoor enthusiasts can show beginners how to be conservation-minded. They can teach them to respect land and wildlife.

GLOSSARY

angler (AN-glur) An angler is a person who fishes. The angler caught fish in the lake.

ecosystem (EE-koh-sis-tem) An ecosystem is a community made up of plants, animals, and their environment. It is important for hunters and anglers to take care of the ecosystem.

ethical (EH-thih-kuhl) Ethical refers to ideas of right and wrong that help influence how people act. Hunters and anglers must make ethical decisions when dealing with animals, the environment, and other people outdoors.

food web (FOOD WEB) A food web is a system of food chains that shows how organisms in a habitat get their food. A food web consists mainly of plants and animals.

lures (LOORZ) Lures are a type of fake bait used to catch fish. Anglers must make sure their lures are securely tied to their fishing lines.

permit (PUR-mit) A permit is written permission to do something. Anglers often need a fishing permit to fish in bodies of fresh water.

shot (SHOT) Shot is a type of small pellet put into a shell that is used as a bullet. Animals that eat lead shot left on the ground can become sick.

stable (STAY-bul) To be stable is to be steady or reliable. Hunting keeps animal populations stable by preventing populations from becoming too large.

state agencies (STAYT AY-jen-seez) State agencies are official government bodies in charge of something. State agencies may be in charge of issuing hunting licenses.

FAST FACTS

- Sportsmanship in the outdoors involves treating nature, animals, and other people with respect.
- Hunting and fishing rules are often created by state agencies or by the National Park Service. Hunters and anglers should follow all rules in their area.
- In most states, hunters and anglers need a permit or license in order to hunt or fish. Hunting is sometimes allowed on private land, but hunters should always get permission to hunt there.
- Some people hunt and fish for food, while others hunt for sport.
- Hunters and anglers should know how to use guns, bows, and fishing rods safely and correctly. They should use legal hunting methods.
- Hunters and anglers should be conservation-minded. They should make ethical choices and avoid leaving equipment, litter, or lead shot behind.

ONE STRIDE FURTHER

- Why is it important to maintain stable animal populations in the wild? What would happen if an animal population became too large or too small?
- Create an "Outdoor Code of Conduct" for hunters or anglers. What five rules would you include? Why?
- Should hunting be considered a sport? Why or why not?

FIND OUT MORE

IN THE LIBRARY

Bell, Samantha S. *Firearm Safety*. Parker, CO: The Child's World, 2024.

Bowman, Chris. *Yellowstone National Park*. Minneapolis, MN: Bellwether Media, Inc., 2023.

Carson, Mary Kay. *Animal Watching*. New York, NY: Odd Dot, 2021.

ON THE WEB

Visit our website for links about outdoor sportsmanship:
childsworld.com/links

Note to Parents, Caregivers, Teachers, and Librarians: We routinely verify our Web links to make sure they are safe and active sites. So encourage your readers to check them out!

INDEX